Inventory

Linda Black

Inventory

Shearsman Books
Exeter

Published in the United Kingdom in 2008 by
Shearsman Books Ltd
58 Velwell Road
Exeter EX4 4LD

www.shearsman.com

ISBN 978-1-905700-90-5

Copyright © Linda Black, 2008.

The right of Linda Black to be identified as the author of this work has been asserted by her in accordance with the Copyrights, Designs and Patents Act of 1988. All rights reserved.

Acknowledgements:
My thanks to Arts Council England and to New Writing Ventures. Many thanks to Mimi Khalvati who sowed the seeds for this project and from whom I have learned so much; to Esther Morgan for her valuable insights, and to Lucy Hamilton for her encouragement.

Some of these poems have appeared in the following publications:
Entering the Tapestry (Enitharmon 2003), *I am Twenty People* (Enitharmon 2007), *Poetry Salzburg Review, Shearsman, Magma,* and in the online journal *Nth Position.*

The cover drawing and internal illustrations are all by the author and are copyright © Linda Black, 2008.

The composition of *Inventory* was funded by Arts Council England.

Contents

Section 1: *Furniture & Things*
Hang up your coat, take of your shoes   15
The box room   16
The yellow chair   17
Here's 'Thin Little Scrap'   18
In the first place you should be comfortably seated   19
I choose a cup   20
Advice to lodgers   22
Custodian   23
Paperclips   24
Misalignment   25
Bed   26
And could it be comfortable   27
Locomotion   28
There is a bell   29
I've a letter to write   30
Memorandum of agreement
entered into this _____ of _____   31

Section 2: *Pictures*
Take my surroundings   37
Between finger and thumb   38
Cushion   39
Think how it could be   40
Hook   41
There's a telephone (667478)   42
The house on the hill   43
Untitled   44
Here is Sadie   45
Unexpected   46
Maze   47
The temporary lamp   48
The question   49

Section 3: *Legs*
    You don't have to explain *everything*   55
    A bentwood chair is out in the garden   56
    The leg fits into the foot   58
    Intentions   59
    A strange thing   60
    Cures for common ailments   61
    My father   63
    I write this   64
    Climbing the stairs   66
    Still he sleeps   67
    She is ironing her hair   68

Section 4: *Garments & Stuff*
    House-mite   73
    In the beginning was a pantry   74
    Maybe   76
    Bananas   77
    Here is your new reference list. Cut it out.   78
    Against the wall   79
    Seamstress   80
    My father is as motionless as one who is asleep   81
    My mother is locked in a jar of ginger   82
    Hints and Tips   83
    Nothing discarded   84
    Such a malcontent   85

Section 5: *Walls, Doors & Windows etc.*
    Door   91
    The abandoned house   92
    When did a wall   93
    She is inside the same space   94
    …when, I open the door   95
    Could it be I mistook tiredness for sadness?   96
    Do you remember?   97
    Badly worn stair treads can be replaced
    with hardboard   98

How the makings of the house	99
Why concoct?	100
What if everything were fixed?	101
It's a mixture of a house	102

For Rosie, Joseph and Thomas

1. Furniture & Things

Inside the Pantry

Hang up your coat, take off your shoes

Your bag will go in the cupboard for safekeeping. What have you got in here, it weighs a ton? I expect you'll be hungry.

He takes it all in: the pantry (one tin of corned beef, 3 eggs, a jar of home-made pickled onions, half a loaf of white bread – uncut, a slab of cheddar and a dish of yellow salted butter); high ceiling (it seems to go all the way to the roof), bare light-bulb, empty vase, single high backed chair, linoleum, Formica, and in a far corner a heavy chenille curtain hiding he suspects the passage to the stairs.

Where can I leave my umbrella?

The box room

On a gate-leg table, an open exercise book (inside, a neatly labelled diagram: the reproductive system of the rabbit – one up from earthworm) and several packets of Trebor mints. Behind sliding glass doors: Beauty (both Black and Sleeping); Jo, Meg, Beth – *a little quiver in her voice* – and Amy; Katy *absolutely on her feet*; Heidi, Raskolnikov. Earthworms, also called 'nightcrawlers', are hermaphroditic and have five pairs of hearts. Dismal days, eventful days, days of commotion.

The yellow chair

Wasn't always, isn't really – underneath it is, as I remember it, a darkish blue, not quite petrel. Scanning the room, I can't find a match and decline to lift its skirt. Three thoughts occur, vie for precedence. I like to be exact, attend to minutiae.

I am mistaken. A petrel is a sea bird, related to the shearwaters, typically flying far from land; the colour (though it isn't) is petrol blue. Small crosses like sideways kisses are woven into the fabric – regularly, but how far apart I couldn't say – and dots, I believe there are dots. I could liken the pattern to swallows – there is something in the curve of a wing.

There are no arms. Its wide back curls around my shoulders, tapers like a cut-off triangle to meet a circular seat. A further point – the springs have gone; under the cover I have placed – some time ago – an old feather cushion and several pieces of thickish card. They slip about sometimes.

Its legs are wooden, hidden. It is my grandmother's chair, a low chair, a feeding chair. I do look later; about some things, I am completely wrong.

Here's 'Thin Little Scrap'

Darting from room to room, bounding stair treads three at a time. He (startlingly male) has a mission, an infrared camera for seeing into the past. What disturbs him is *he can't remember where he put it*. The clothes-airer when she wasn't looking? The laundry basket? Which might mean it ended up through the mangle. Surreptitiously he backtracks, keeping out of harm's way. Last month it was here, two years ago there. *Where was I last October?* His concern is no one else finds it, tainting it with their perceptions. Oh, he's tried collaboration (female, nuff said). He feels a creak in the bone, due he thinks to rapid reversals – or could it be the angle of jump? There's a tune going round in his head. He blames the Mike Sammes Singers. If he weren't trapped here, he'd be after them with his broom and his cotton cloth (dipped in gumption), this tinker, this grudge, this ne'er-do-well.

In the first place, you should be comfortably seated

With the removal of the alimentary canal, a general impression of the reproductive organs is at once apparent. Two sac-like bodies lie above the nerve cord. The two ovaries, white, translucent, triangular bodies, can be seen attached to the posterior face of the septum between segments 12 and 13. Their size will depend on their ripeness. You will notice that no attempt has been made to display the testes. Is everything clear? Is there any difficulty?

I choose a cup

One blue, one green – one missing (the same in all ways but one, *which* I can't clearly say). Two matching saucers: blue cup, green saucer, green cup, blue saucer. Nothing else resonates, particularly not the colour of tea. I found (?) a broken cup some time ago under the sink, my sink.

Do I throw it out? Pretty, delicate, hand painted; part damaged, part not – does the bit that is signal death to the bit that isn't, then the bit that wasn't, won't be? Is it inevitable, the flawed part dragging down the rest? If I broke my arm would you throw me out? What about craftsmanship, beauty, the right to be – to not be perfect; for each part to play its part – to carry on – to fall apart? For the sake of a blemish should the rest suffer? Through no fault of its own. How does it offend? It hasn't changed. Lessened by association . . . and so forth.

I am looking at a china coffee cup from the days of crystal cruets, monogrammed napkin-rings, crumb-trays. It is white, hand painted, rimmed in gold leaf as is the handle and decorated with curlicues and borders of differing blue stripes. A crack runs the circumference of the base and up one side. Visible from the outside only, placed at regular intervals, are four rivets, slightly disguised.

Printed on the base: *325* (in gold) *Royal Winton* MADE IN ENGLAND A and what looks like ELEANUM, smaller, in blue, rather faded; floral pattern, handle cross-riveted at the top, pinned at the base – right the way through. For this, I like it all the more.

Round the corner from where I used to live (when I lived there) I once rescued smithereens of china – jugs, tureen lids, clay pipes, the like – from a deep hole, as many as I could. I keep them in a shoebox, show visitors.

Post Script

It was a riveting story.

All eyes were riveted on her

The grip was firm enough to rivet her to the spot.

Advice to lodgers

A lodger has the right to use the knocker and the doorbell. He cannot claim to affix a plate. Persons who take rooms will be prudent to make various inquiries as to the character of the house. People must live somewhere. It is especially annoying if the lodger finds that through his want of caution his goods are distrained. In the metropolis there are springing up blocks of buildings with a common stair. They are mentioned here as a sort of compromise. Some people are violently prejudiced against lodging-house keepers. Lodgers must have free ingress and egress, and should possess a latchkey. They should have keys also to their rooms, cupboards, boxes, drawers &c., and should use them and not leave them about as temptation. They should of course be models of regularity. Perhaps their discontent and misery are as often due to themselves.

Custodian

Mind me. I am the keeper of the cracks, the server of thin air. I note how the dust sits, how breath creases, folds inwards. I log the spaces, the bounty of nothing; inspect the angle of each or every shadow. I heed where a lip leaves its mark, a footprint crosses an empty table, a hollow where a head once lay and then I wipe it away. Dents do not escape me, nor welts, straps, ridges. I record it all. Punctiliously, for all my wayward ways.

Paperclips

A woman I hardly knew came round once and gave me a large tray of bedding plants. Then she gave me a box of coloured paperclips. I tried to hang on to them. If I needed one I'd search instead for the ordinary metal kind, disentangle one from the chain down the stairwell.

Misalignment

Daily he drags closed the doors that do not shut; the old man with the arched back, ties string around handles, hammers flat protruding nails. He angles his closed eyes downward towards his navel. He can't get his words to match his thoughts. In the box- room, he begs for clemency.

Bed

I approach my bed from a different direction as though it will make a difference, leave via the right, returning by the same path. Dark isn't, so I can see my way. I keep my head down to remain befuddled. I shiver. I have to read the clock then double check. I lie back down and silently count the hours – it goes like this: twelve to one – one, one to two – two, two to three – three, and so on, depending where I start and end. Then I count what's left. I use my fingers without moving, acknowledge each in turn, mentally feeling. Sometimes I have the strange sensation they aren't all there. I notice if there's a gap in the curtains. If there is, I do nothing. On the right side, there are no sharp corners; on the left is the hole.

And could it be comfortable?

What makes comfort? Bed – no. Chair – which chair? Hard chair, temporary chair – for eating, reading the paper spread out over the kitchen table? An on-the-way-to chair, a just-doing-this-and-then chair. Garden bench? – a sit-down-for-two-seconds bench, a glass of water, a plate of some small food. Anna is sitting reading a book. Anna's chair is a white plastic 'lounger' with a padded seat. Comfortable, she says. Other people's sofas look comfortable. There's the room for watching T.V, the garden for relaxing, bed for sleep – in theory. Comfort is from the inside – you either have it or you don't. Don't you read in the bathtub?' she says.

Locomotion

Only degenerate animals are sedentary or parasitic. One is apt to consider worms as rather sluggish. Their ability to withdraw into their burrows with amazing rapidity (violent movements called escape movements) makes it necessary to be very quick in one's attempt to catch them. For general purposes, earthworms are best immersed in 30% or 50% spirit until they are dead.

There is a bell

But no one sees it – it blends too well into the paint. A bell should be a harebell, the best kind of bell to be, nodding on a cotton thin stem; a pixie hat for each, translucent, lit by fairy light.

I've a letter to write

It could go something like this:

I've had these for sometime, in the small drawer in my old desk… I am sidetracked by the desk – tempted to explain that 'small' means about five inches wide, that the handle is made of bone, to itemise the contents, tell how the lid is always open…

I'm sending you these. I've had them for some time wrapped in a bit of polythene, spares from a gift I gave my sister. One could say I should have given them too. I just thought the likelihood of her needing them remote, so I kept them, not in case I needed them but because I knew you did. I remember when we bought ours. I remember when yours broke, that I wanted you to have it mended. It was a few years ago now and I expect you've learnt to live without it.

Memorandum of Agreement entered into this _____ of _____

The said _____ hereby agrees to let, and the said _____ hereby agrees to rent and take all those rooms on the _____ floor (or floors) of the house of the said _____ situate and being No._____, _____ street (or as the case may be), in the parish of _____ in the county of _____. And the said _____ hereby agrees to leave on the premises hereby agreed to be let, at the termination of the tenancy hereby created, all the easements, appurtenances, furniture, effects, and other things severally set forth and enumerated in the inventory hereto annexed and which are now in or upon the said premises and are the property of the said _____ and also all the glass windows whole and unbroken.

2. Pictures

Over the Silver Shoes

Take my surroundings:

This accumulation. I wish to examine how it (collective or singular?) came to be. (Already there exists an assumption of *passivity*.) The mind balks at such a colossal task; fear not – a methodical approach renders the most complex of situations a piece of piss. Having assembled, it is thus possible to deconstruct. 'Surroundings' in this instant, refers to a room known as 'the studio' – a rather misleading epithet as the room itself is devoid of natural light depending for purposes within upon borrowed light (somewhat sparse) from the hallway and in turn from the upper landing (and a fraction perchance from the pane above the front door?). Have I not heard it said the last to arrive is the first to go? I have said so myself. Ah, but to know what was (or is) last? Do not be unduly concerned – there are precautions quite within one's grasp.

Between finger and thumb

Think of the word *abracadabra* – now picture the hand movements: conjuring, coaxing – a slow pull backwards through thick air as though grasping a fine but invisible thread tightly between finger and thumb. Or the pulling of a single hair with relish; a look of glee, a mask of evil. To achieve the desired affect the thread must, of course, be attached to something living, feeling, subjugated. Nothing sudden happens here – no yanking, no gross movements – all is in the stance, the poise of delivery, the very doing. Not that this *action*, this *doing* can be said to be in any way ponderous. The desire is measured; the extraction savoured. Of the persecutor, little is known.

Take this description, not of a drawing, but of the *memory* of a drawing executed some time ago, in pencil, in an exercise book, on unlined paper: A woman is walking along a street – of this I am sure, though no road, kerb or pavement is visible. She is wearing a winter coat, belted at the waist and a hat, possibly of wool – let us say she is well wrapped up. She is neither young, nor sinister. We approach her from the back. Trailing behind her, on a leash, are two hind legs, not animal but human. The leash is held between finger and thumb. If it is not, it *ought* to be.

Cushion

I'm torn, as is this cushion – one frayed hole in exactly the centre of a tulip. The weave is open, giving curves – edges of leaves, flowers in cameo, curlicues – a slight serrated look like cross stitch but more subtle. I am pulled like a thread into the design. Its history is more appealing, and the spot, *two* spots, of blue paint, not their nature, that they are there. These, speaking broadly, I know about, though I couldn't cite shade or number. The fabric came from curtains used thoughtlessly as dustsheets, rescued unlike the friendship. Lately I've taken to removing this cushion and two others, similar but smaller, putting them out of sight.

Think how it could be

An open casement, curtains spotted and flapping (it's easy to draw spots), fresh picked flowers, a kettle on the boil – I'm peering in – elves like busy bees, darning socks – or would it be mice? – an uninterrupted expanse of floorboards; a place where the Hoover can glide. I hate people seeing in to me.

Hook

Begin with a hook (presuppose a surface of blackened wax, a sharpened tool, a certain dedication) …replace the hook with a fine-pointed nail, eyeing the spot to penetrate.

A question mark hangs over the nail, becomes embedded, becomes a hanger, but not for coats. Metal or wooden or bandaged in silk – used, discarded, acquired, their shallow arcs suspend the inanimate.

A small opening, a bodice fitted to the flesh, sleeves for thin arms, a tiny waist, lengthening… lengthening… wending its way – a dress seeking a child, a dress unfit.

A pattern repeated. Another nail, another hanger, a floorboard or two, a sprinkling of powder, the leaving in haste – the corner of a bed, worn and worried.

If clothes can feign sadness this one does; so flimsy it can hardly compose itself, it weeps from the hanger, bodiless; the shame of a missing button, a stain, a broken zip; an unholy wisp, unhoped-for.

Water gives energy; here there is none – nor sunlight – and so far to go. How easy to replicate nails, narrowing the spaces between (wasn't I taught to observe their existence); to cut out, like the next one wasn't.

Needled and cross-stitched, hatched into shadow – half in, half out – a petticoat withdraws, skirts the undertow, slips stitches, slender straps hardly hanging on.

There's a telephone (667478)

But it's a party line; when she picks it up she hears the next-door neighbours in the middle of a conversation.

She makes models with rubber moulds; bunnies, plaster of Paris gnomes, paints their clothes, their little faces. If they have too many air bubbles she throws them away.

At night, she leans out of the window and whistles (as best she can): *whu-whu whu-whu whoo-whoo.*

The house on the hill

Is hard to see – the harder the better. I believe in struggle (though I'm tempted by laser correction): the honing of a better person, a soul fit for a second life. I half recall a diagram: a section through rock. Slate is elevated to rooftop; sediment crumbles to nothing. A river bursts its banks; odds caught in the flow are battered by rocks, randomly thrown off course, no longer part of the ebb of it all. On the surface, little beings (indistinguishable though each is different) shuffle round and round – there they go wittering on. Sometimes they are still, fall silent. When one drops off it's hardly noticed, there's always someone to pick up the baton.

Untitled

Granted it should in some way hang together. I have been bitten – on the right shoulder. At first, I thought my beauty spot had overgrown, making me less not more. On the wall behind: *The Cato Street Conspirators*, '…*on the memorable night of the 23rd of Feb 1820 at the moment when Smithers the Police officer was stabbed…*' To the right of the Cruickshanks is a Gorey. A man and woman dance together. Sideways. She is wearing an outrageous feathered hat, almost a creature. Her dress wreathes around her body up to her neck; a long-gloved arm snakes across her partner's shoulder; curtains fall in folds, slither along a floor more like blades of grass. There are shadows. His suit is white. There are some things I didn't mention – a champagne glass, a spidery chair, that it is numbered and signed, but not dated. My heart sinks.

Here is Sadie

In a home, back from the dead. (No more holidays in Blackpool for the partially sighted.) Sadie with the big hair. Little-old-lady Sadie who remembered everyone's birthdays till she couldn't see to write, telling me again; 'Your daddy, ooh he was a lovely fella!' My daddy 'The Ginger Beer Man', delivering the lemonade on a Thursday in his horse and cart, coming back on the Sunday for his tuppence and a cup of tea. 'Ours-was-the-last-house'- Sadie. Anne comes every day to dress Sadie. Anne is sick and miserable. Mother and daughter don't get on. Anne's husband was weasly Maurice, executor of my father's will. (In this way he procured my mother's cocktail cabinet, Venetian glass, place mats, nest of tables and all her money.) My grandfather was a Maurice but called Mon. My brother-in-law is a Morris. Morris's mother was a Doris like my mother Doris. Morris and my sister (known by her second name) were given an old framed ad of a Morris Minor inscribed 'You'll be glad you married a Morris'.

Unexpected

I think back *(think* being what I do, *back* being how I do it). Of course, a proportion of my thinking will be forwards (is time running out, what will I wear) though not forward-thinking. This particular back thinking is not related – as far as I can tell – to any personal trauma, but to a page in an old notebook. As I recall, something to do with a back door, a tray and a striped dress. (I can picture the fabric). After trawling pages, I find it. Here it is, as it was:

Outside the back door of J's house is a garden. No ordinary suburban garden, it has rocks – some quite high so you can't see beyond – established plants and pools of water where you might expect to see lawn. And here the washing hangs on lines which stoop so low in places it touches the ground. A crepe dress, vertical stripes, buttons down the front, lies spread-eagled on a rock. It is not my house, not my job to bring in the washing. I feel I ought, though I don't. Instead I pick up a bunch of greens from a ledge just outside the door, bring them in. I have some sliced rye bread on a tray, just a few pieces. I feel tempted to spread the tiny crust thick with butter. I carry (also) a box of crayons. I will go about *my* tasks – the rest is not to do with me.

I learnt this at school: *Towards the end of summer on the under surface of a leaf, Dryopteris or bracken develops a kidney shaped structure called 'sori'.*

Maze

I've an etching, one of a series, loosely based on Pandora. A woman kneels on the earth, head in hands, above her in the sky a fine tangle; a knot of ribbons so interlocked it is impossible to unravel. Clearly, a pretty burden. In another she sits on a sofa, hands folded in her lap; lightning streaks across her face, a crevasse opening beside her. In yet another she is seated on a high stool, her long hair plaited and crossed at the ends like an open pair of scissors, across her thighs, a cat-o'-nine-tails. Beside her on the dressing table, perfume bottles, sharp and angled, a pair of evening gloves almost alive; in the mirror she faces, naught but a passing cloud.

The temporary lamp

The temporary lamp highlights the low ceiling so I'm drawn to noticing the stain where the washing machine leaked. I have drawn a pencil line around it in the hope of keeping it contained. I flash through how to conceal it, get the job done really fast, an oil-based undercoat, a touch of emulsion. One stain leads to another. Where the entrance has been narrowed a substance seeps from the bricks causing the paint to flake away. The one in Joseph's room above his empty bed is a dark cloud in a watercolour landscape; the edges bleed and fade. Below the window, the plaster is swollen and pockmarks through the creaminess like curdled milk.

The question

The assumes only one, *but* ask ten people in a room to draw a box (as once I did – though there were more than ten, though they were not in all accuracy people as we think of people, being of an age younger than the descriptor indicates) and no two shall be found to be identical. Trust me for I have no proof, save of my own certainty. Is it true to say – can one say – a question once sidetracked (see above) remains a question? I can say anything. Have I not already done so? And so one question gives way to another. Would it be better (as judged by whom?) to return to boxes? This is how it goes (begins): (to start with knowing that a start is a beginning is surely to start with more than a beginning – here, *I* already know the end and can choose whether to keep it to myself.) (Voice wants concrete, says *must have*) To get to point A, one goes through many false starts, delaying gratification: A blank sheet of sugar paper, some sort of drawing implement (not charcoal). Instruction: Draw a box. No one begins. Question: Where should I begin? Simultaneous question: How big?

Eventual outcome: 30ish boxes of differing sizes, shapes, proportions, perspectives, all false starts.

3. Legs

How she dances!

You don't have to explain *everything*

If you say, for example 'his leg was *still* in plaster' it's enough that someone knows how it came to be (his mother, say). It's enough to see a field of buttercups without knowing their precise position, what lies between, how they came to be, exactly when they will expire.

A bentwood chair is out in the garden

(As if it upped and wandered) its seat dipped and splintered. *And the sun shall not heal...* O to sit on an imaginary (but one – a corner of – *is* known to me, is *almost* a reality... I think of porches, a porch, *the* porch, a frosted glass enclosure, *encasement,* through which for some time I'd no choice but to pass) verandah, swinging my legs. Each chair I own is more or less uncomfortable; each dictates to me my thoughts.

Is she reaching out or turning away? Younger she is than I am now... *younger than springtime ...something... than laughter...* I am dressed in white kid boots – I assume it was she tied the laces. What is 'kid' – is it like veal, pale with white blood, starved of light? And only part of her. Was it necessary, each step across the verandah; a right of passage, feet off ground, a small soul slightly elevated? And above that and above that... up one staircase and then another... towards the eves... attic... gabled roof... higher... higher. The harder to be rooted. And then came the bolder shoe, the longed for height, toes forced into shoes with heels that spike. The further from. The out of reach.

But I've got there too soon. Shall I go back? Add a scene in which a mother is a mother and a daughter is good enough? *Or* one where a father (*Lindy! Sandy! Late for school!*) calls the wicked uncle to stop them fight, *or* where a powerless father puts an arm around a weeping daughter, *or* where the daughter sits on the stairs banging her head against the wall?

(You may think she was a mother of real flesh and blood, that the child with the finger in her mouth – what does it mean, that she placed her finger so, standing as she was on the veranda looking out over the balustrade down to whoever looked up at her? – was me. Is it insignificant that I think I recognise, through the veneer, through the leaded lights, through the reflection of an arch and a spindly tree, the swirled pattern on the curtains, of no consequence the gap between rail and strut? Stave, lintel, pillar – pane, paling, newel-post – each piece of timber, each endangered brick, each portion of her, each cell, petrified.)

Verandah gives way to porch. By this time we don't talk or remember how or ever having done so. Each day has its routine: how to sit, how not to, how to place a knife and fork when food is done, how precisely to fold a shirt. Do you still have that picture of me – the one 'not how you wanted me to be?' I have it too. Such a neat cursive script, such well formed letters – you could have been a teacher. You must have had some friends.

The leg fits into the foot

And not the foot into the leg. The toe must not be allowed to drop into a downward position. A rough knee joint will very quickly wear a hole in the trouser. The shoulder joint may need some explanation. Movement of the head can be got by rocking – up one end, down the other. As time goes by you will discover new movements and forms of expression. Only a fringe of hair is attached to the head. Garments are not made to come off and on.

Intentions

She is thinking about ironing. She has no recollection of putting up the ironing board. It's been up (she thinks) since the night next door. I don't know why I thought that, she thinks, but lets it pass. The phrase 'she was ironing in an upstairs room' holds a certain attraction, though, as the practicality is too much for her, she decides to leave it in its usual place, slightly re-angled. She is struggling with the cover – *now* she knows why it began as 'up'. What infuriates her is when someone else puts it back upside down and the cover falls three-quarters of the way off (plus that bit underneath – the padding; how do you call it? No, no word comes – wouldn't it have been asbestos in days gone by?). Twice the problem. And harder still to get out because of the bucket. Fabric and metal just don't marry and invariably the drawstring doesn't and you have to fiddle with it to make any sense. Board, of course, implies wood. She'd enjoy ironing then. Something stable to dig a pin into.

A strange thing

Quite possibly, most probably – I would say definitely – I am about to misquote Ionesco:

'Donald's little girl has one red eye and one green eye and Elizabeth's little girl has one green eye and one red eye, but whereas it's the left eye of Donald's little girl that's red and the right eye that's green, it's the right eye of Elizabeth's little girl that's red and the left eye that's green.'

Could have been blue. I *think* (by which I mean I don't *know*) that my mother had an infected toenail. So do I; cured temporarily with a concoction (one part oil to five parts tincture) from the Royal London Homeopathic Hospital, applied every day for the first few weeks, then three times a week, then once. There's a bit left in a galvanised tin box under the bath.

It's a strange thing . . . but I don't rightly know how . . . or if it always was, or which one . . . like I made it up (unlike the bucket under the stairs) . . . buried stuff, *Fiddler on the Roof* stuff like I watched recently on TV missing the first half – my whole family, even my grandfather, at the cinema – the tears he cried for all he never spoke of. Who were they – who was she, my namesake?

.... that my father was
  – *was* – blind in one eye.

Could also include:

Eyeglass in a leather pouch – how it swung out, attached at a corner. Glasses with one lens blanked. His crippled legs – some sort of accident (to his hip?) – when he worked for Pathe News? – as a runner? – before I was born? Why do I think of a double-decker bus? Wasn't it trams in those days? How he cringed with pain but never complained. Callipers. Pills. His bad stomach.

My poor dad.

NB. Can tin be galvanised?

Cures for common ailments

A poultice of crumb of bread seeped in vinegar will cure a new corn in one night. A little plaster of Paris damped in paste will answer the same purpose, as will a small circle, pierced in the centre, of agaric, or touchwood (from the touchwood tree). Crushed leaves of bindweed applied to styes are very efficacious. Many people use little sticks of butter or cocoa as a cosmetic. If a little cocaine is added and a sting rubbed with the stick, it will procure immediate relief. Hay fever (what an infliction!) is an indisposition that concerns us for it makes the sufferer look ugly and almost ridiculous. No beauty can withstand it. It should be struggled against from the beginning. Once the evil of an in-growing toenail is there, the question is how to cure it. Wet the whole foot. Apply a solution of gutta-percha (80 parts) and chloroform (10 parts). The flesh is thus rendered hard and insensitive.

My father

My father had six fingers, a hooked nose and one eye. My father had a hinged jaw and no teeth, a dewdrop and a pack of Woodbines. My father had a gold signet ring, swollen knuckles and his hands were claws. My father wore braces and shat in a bucket under the stairs. My father sat on a low stool lighting the boiler for hours. He sat on a high stool eating bananas and bread. My father had a mother but I did not know her. My father had a father but I did not know him. My father had a grey paisley scarf. My father made tea for my mother. But I did not know her. My father took me to the playground in Potternewton Park. This was before he had an iron leg. I spun round and round. My mother milked my father. My father opened the door to 'uncle' Charlie. My father nodded and shuffled. My mother's stepmother liked my father. She told me this in a car outside Chislehurst caves. She said it was a bad match. My mother told me 'I want never gets'. If he were here I think he would be standing, staring at nothing. I think he would be leaning backwards. I think he would look like he might fall over. My father had hollow legs.

I write this:

*Dust, in the crannies of carved leaves, white
against the darkness of wood, settled in spaces.*

*Legs are carved totems, exotic stems bare
no fruit where no birds fly.*

*Significance, losing ground, retreats
to the corner, sulks.*

*On bright days, when imperfections glow – one
may not mind or then one might.*

*Here, moods change, but the table
remains the same, growing old passively.*

I read it to a friend. It's about spaces, she says. So, I write this:

*Dust, in the crannies of carved leaves, white
against the darkness of wood, <u>settled in spaces</u>*

*For legs, carved totems: exotic stems bearing
no fruit where no birds fly and grief <u>wings space</u>.*

*Significance, losing ground, retreats
to the corner, sidling in <u>shadowed space.</u>*

*On bright days, imperfections glow
– one may grow to loath the <u>fallow space.</u>*

*Here, moods change, but the table
remains the same, passive in <u>wasted space.</u>*

Receive various feedback: starts really well – soon as you lose concrete embodiment, too abstract – need *examples* of imperfections, *images* of significance – didn't want to know it was a table – go with the birds that don't fly – where does *fallow* come from? Where indeed. Remove 'grief' so: 'birds fly *in distant space*'; add 'significance *of twigs…*' replace the 'fallow' line with '*these cloven feet claw empty space*'. Receive further feedback: is it a *real* twig? – the spaces are all the same – try repeating the *same* refrain – like the shifting angles – focus it – add 'I' to the last couplet – think about the emotional life – bleak language, verging on brutal – impotence – claustrophobic – closed off – sense of dead foliage; *The Grecian Urn* – like best '*fallow space*' . . .

It stands in the corner like something unseen, like the dust, by an exposed brick wall – darkly next to dark, the only place for it. I gave it to my sister. She gave it back. I didn't buy it, choose it. My mother did. (Three weighted words.) I can't place where it stood or what was on it. It shares the same darkness, from the same dark hallway.

I'd like to sleep now, go away.

Climbing the stairs

Eyes closed; embossed wallpaper, punched from the inside – the over and over of it. Nothing but ringing, ringing. Under the bed – what one sleeps on top of! Lips. I liked his thigh. It took a long time to blow the candle out – the effort, the huff of it.

Still he sleeps

When he was younger she'd creep in, lean over close to his face, check – is he breathing? Kicked off shoes in the hallway, yesterday's juice on the sitting room table. He loves tomatoes. They said she had a gritty placenta. Not premature – pre-term. His second-to-last last day – he leaves *everything* to the last minute. His fingernails were perfectly formed, perfectly formed. The malaria tablets make his head ache. When he's out late she leaves the outside light on. It shines up through the gaps in the floorboards. He limps without a built-up shoe.

She is ironing her hair

Over brown paper, washed first and rinsed in vinegar. She has to bend the level of the ironing board. Her body feels cumbersome – more so because of the heat. If one were only one's intelligence, she thinks – no, that won't do. I am neither past, present, or future. In the dark house, the heart shuts down.

4. Garments & Stuff

Inside the Box

House mite

All the usual accompaniments; tinkling bell, voluminous ears...
my clothes are specially made (I know a little mouse). I have my
favourite places – the rhubarb patch, the folds of a handkerchief.
Your house is my palace. Wherever you go so do I. I dodge and
follow. I climb sash cords; unpick hems, mix salt and sugar. I
pray for you.

In the beginning was a pantry

I'm looking now at what was inside – quite a lot of the usual stuff like jam, sage, nuts. At the time I made a long list, handwritten with dip pen and black ink and think it worth noting *all* was contained in bottles, too many to replicate here but if I say... bottles of flax, bottles of dice, bottles of coffin... Some things, such as an opened pie, eardrops, a decanter of ox-blood and a couple of Toby Jugs, I didn't list.

The pantry looked out onto a room, but not a kitchen. The perspective, from the inside – the back of the top shelf – makes the protagonist very small, fairy-like even, and by the end she certainly has wings. To the room. Not much to say really apart from a ceiling covered in 40-watt light bulbs, a floor awash with silver shoes (the type you get on wedding cakes) and a small door at the other end.

Simultaneously, out of the ox-blood climbs a little man, *he*. Out of a bottle of fingernails, *she*, mentioned earlier. Both are unclothed, apart from something wispy and not very discernible and her black high heels, and slightly androgynous. If you can be slightly. How they get down is a little uncertain – he helps her? She helps him? They hold hands and jump? Have they made a previous arrangement or is this serendipity? Either way, they make for the door as they would, though with some difficulty as proportionately the shoes are about half their size. At this point, on reflection, I would say if not hope, anticipation (along with a cloud of flying lips, akin to birds) is in the air.

Not having measured the size of the room, it is arbitrary how long it takes to reach the door. They could stumble; build their relationship. They do reach the door, and as if it knew they were coming it opens, slowly – oh and silently (creaking would give altogether the wrong expectation.) A hand appears – loomingly? – or in a flash? (no mention of an arm); on the end of each finger a silver shoe sparkles... enticing... mesmerising. Then come the strings – how she dances!

He (the man) is dark and sombre. Somehow or other he has found the time to change into a black suit – thin lapels, handkerchief in the top pocket, bow tie, hands by his sides, legs stuck together. Everything darkens. *He* is everywhere, watching: inside a wine glass, under the sewing machine, sunk in a tin of shoe polish, and so forth. In the distance a sound can be heard, a buzzing, faint at first, then louder... *louder*... nearer... *nearer*...

Is anyone or anybody interchangeable? Is it to do with emphasis, tone of voice? Is anyone there? Can anybody help?

Maybe

Maybe not. I've a few things to see to first – that stain on my skirt. I saw a girl yesterday, stood there right on the corner by the main road, bold as brass, arms up in the air, her body, the whole of it, yawning wide – in broad daylight. Salt would've done it but you have to act quick, no dallying. Funny how the slightest things put you off. Used to be white socks and string vests. I'd be sitting there on the end of J's mum's bed watching her uncurl each roller one by one; back-comb, smooth, lacquer, thinking 'please God let her hair be OK so we can go out'. It was something about the way he dressed – the wet patch on the back of his shirt – he wasn't bad looking, just sloppy. Soaking's good for stains, but the water has to be cold otherwise they set. It's the same with milk. Milk's a coagulant.

Bananas

Some things I like about bananas, some I don't. I like eating them, not the effort of opening them, their in-between-soft-and-hardness not the stringy bits down the side. I kept two recently till beyond their prime.

Some things have no use – spent batteries, struck matches (stick them in an apple-core, watch them burn) old brass curtain hooks...

...a short pair, a long pair, a matching bedspread, homemade (by whom?) in a bag under the bed. I think of edges, how pleasantly the selvage runs white down the length, printed sometimes with name, number, palette...

...two odd shoulder pads, a card of *World Famous* hooks and eyes – some used, some hanging off; a label, also of card – *All Cotton Gingham Fast Colours Made In England*, on the reverse *Bleached And Pre-Shrunk No Special Treatment Necessary*; a crochet hook, left over wool and underneath, two plastic angels clashing their symbols, conducting the heavens...

...a hinged hairpin once used for perms... two cotton-less, wooden reels (*Sylko Three Shells; 100 yards Mercerised Machine Twist; Lemon and Dk Cardinal – shade 29*)

....my grandmother at her treadle... treadle, treadle, treadle...

Here is your new reference list. Cut it out.

Single textured Macintosh, raincoat overcoat, cape, cloak
  –unlined or saddle lined –other than woollen, leather or fur
Macintosh, cape, raincoat –other than those above ... ...
Overcoat lining (detached) ... ...
Jacket, blazer, bolero, blouse-type jacket –if lined and not
  woollen, leather or fur ... ...
Jacket (including blouse), blazer –other than those in the
  two categories above ... ...
Cardigan, sweater, jersey, jumper, pullover, waist-coat –with
  long sleeves, and woollen, leather or fur ... ...
Waistcoat, jumper, jersey, sweater, cardigan –other than
  those in previous item ... ...
Shirt † –if woollen ... ...
Shirt † –other than woollen ... ...
Blouse, shirt-blouse, shawl –if woollen... ... ...
Blouse, shirt-blouse, shawl –other than woollen... ... ...
Trousers, slacks, over-trousers, breeches –if woollen... ... ...
Trousers, slacks, over-trousers, breeches –other than woollen
Skirt, divided skirt –if woollen ... ...
Skirt, divided skirt –other than woollen... ... ...
Pyjama suit, nightshirt, combinations –if woollen ... ...
Combinations –other than woollen... ... ...
Woollen vest; non-woollen vest with sleeves; woollen pants
  or trunks; non-woollen pants (long legs) ... ...
Undergarment not elsewhere listed ... ...
Pair of stockings, socks, bathing trunks –if woollen... ... ...
Pair of socks –other than woollen; cotton swimming drawers
4 handkerchiefs (each of area less than 1sq ft) ... ...
2 *other* handkerchiefs (less than 2ft in length or breadth)... ...

† *with or without collars attached*

Against the wall

I write leaning against a wall – not stone but plasterboard, smoothly painted, the colour *Camargue* – just by the architrave of an open door. Any moment I will need to make a move, turn off the water, avert disaster. Yesterday I declined to buy the paper with the full, bloodied face, though it doesn't stop me thinking of it. To be precise, only my left shoulder blade is touching – a pose which could become uncomfortable. On the right-hand ledge of the window opposite, I can almost make something out – fabric, red and orange – a child's tee shirt? I've been watching it for days. They print a photo of a family's children the day after, as they were the day before.

Seamstress

She has thread (but no needle) pre-cut into strands of equal length. She has scored an apple into segments; through each she pulls a thread. They dangle like the ribbons of a maypole. She knots the ends. She halves then quarters the lace circle of a tablecloth, cuts the corner to leave a hole the size of her waist. She joins serviettes and handkerchiefs, adds a zip; they hang in points around her ankles. She takes a paper napkin, spreads it out and refolds into a rectangle. Tearing skilfully, she opens it out – 'There, a dolman sleeve'.

My father is as motionless as one who is asleep

And in the state of paralysis. My father is inert, as if he could be lifted in one piece and would not bend. My father is swaddled in a cocoon or wrapped in bandages. As if he has lain long in his nest. It has taken some time to notice his stillness. To see he is there. From sunset to sunset he has lain in his wraps, unable – as I now see – to withstand the journey. We must call a physician – of *his* race, *his* people. Have we been callous? My father requests a comb, which I do not have and all my venturing will not provide. For a moment he has risen, is propped upright. I admire the cloth of his tailored suit. I love my father, this little man, shrivelled to the smallest of beings.

My mother is locked in a jar of ginger

I hear her battling with the lid, trying to hump herself out of the sickly liquid. It suits me not to let her out. I hear her invective – 'shite' and 'bugger'. I shall continue to disappoint. Her suspender is stuck; she is tugging at her roll-on. Let's have some music, something with a thump to it.

Hints and Tips

Pillows stuffed with camel's hair and covered with the skin of the same animal are useful against insomnia. Nothing is better than a lemon for cleaning nails. Stick the ends of the fingers into it and turn. If pearls are shut up with a piece of ash root, it prevents them losing their colour. Should wiseacres laugh, let them laugh. A feminine arm should be round and white. Those who have thin arms can soon increase their size by energetic friction. Cigar boxes are the best receptacles you can choose for your feathers. When a foot is well made, boots and shoes wear well. Cover an old brandy barrel with pleated retonne trimmed with brown guipure. Wrap up your woollens in linen and place them inside. It will not look amiss in the corner with a pretty plant on top. If your fingers are square and wide, you may narrow them a little by pinching and squeezing the tips. Needless to say, you will not obtain tapered fingers at once.

Nothing discarded

Not a broken iron, a dried up paint pot. Socks and pants ironed. Each piece of clothing neatly folded in a plastic bag. Boxes and boxes of her unworn shoes I gave away.

I'm trying really hard to wear my new boots.

Such a malcontent

I'm thinking *habitual*. (I'm writing in the sky right now – a thin attempt to break free.) *Habit*: (rhymes with rabbit). Ingrained. Over and over. A long, loose garment not easy to get rid of. *Habitual* – a giving up – or an inability to, very different from 'regular' or 'periodic'. To *inhabit* – home, mind, body (the latter one can despise, lament or nurture.) She had *habituated* the chimps to humans. *Habitat, habitation* (signs of): one's nest, full of life's trappings, one's place of rest.

5. Walls, Doors & Windows etc.

A buzzing . . . faint at first

Door

I like this door. I've always liked this door, particularly the cracks where the wood has split slightly – maybe as a result of the central heating – the creamy, understated non-colour of the paint, the panels, plain like an upstairs attic door, a servant's door. The doorway is narrower than most so the door has been cut to fit. The lower panels are shorter, as is the custom with doors. The handle, of white porcelain, is missing a grub screw. There's a small gap at the side of one of the panels and traces of filler I'm tempted to pick at, scrape away. Approaching it visually from a distance causes me to observe the lines of perspective, how the angles relate to the adjacent wall, the corner. There's a thin shadow where one wall meets another, obliterated where the light is brightest so there's almost no distinction between adjoining walls and I could almost believe it an area of flatness. When the door is closed and the light off it's almost pitch black in here.

The abandoned house

Naturally, she chooses the back – gate, dustbin, poison tree: some pile on the right, looking from the kitchen window (see, she's inside and out). A mound of earth. Now she's peering down from her old bedroom and it's dusk and those men are there – davening, expunging ghosts. Shoo! Shoo! No bodies buried here.

The laburnum is nearer to the house. Slabs (so much easier to manage) and borders are overgrown with grass. Actually, no – let's have dog roses, briars, macranthas, something with thorns fitting for 'Château Despair'. The coalhole. Wasp traps on the window ledge. (Ahh – summer!) Fly paper. *What's brown and ticks on walls? Brown ticky paper!*

Steps up – not many – two – three. *Use your stick.* A pose in a party dress. *This tea's like dishwater.*

When did a wall

Become not enough? Tapestries, hangings, lime-wash, distemper, straight onto a porous surface; the introduction of colour – a base and a pigment. Work the paint down and across, spreading out from the centre in squares like a giant chess board so the edges of one square blend with the edges of the next. Paint that is poorly applied eventually flakes. Can you blame this whoever-it-was for rushing the job? – perhaps they'd better things to do or it's just not in their make up; the sort who'd throw food on a plate, cabbage half on, half off.

She *is* inside the same space

It's just the parameters are wider. Walls she can circumnavigate, though she may have to go out of her way. She can travel by bus, but not up or under. She's not too bad balancing on a stepladder reaching for a tendril. Water is a different matter.

...when, I open the door

and see them standing there. I look over their shoulders and there *is* a back gate and it *is* open. I offer them water and crumbs. I sit on the stoop. Did they see the plants up there? Moments ago, a laden window box drifted across the welkin close to the upstairs window, *inches away*, hovered a while then plummeted. No one cried out.

Could it be I mistook sadness for tiredness?

The droopy windows. (There was once a man, a noted conductor, who lost the ability to sleep. At first they thought it a period of insomnia – his wife moved out of the bedroom, the doctors did all they could, but eventually he died.) A house can appear to be stable. A sudden storm, a violent wind and off it might go, no saying where. (It wouldn't be the first.) To move a fridge without emptying isn't sensible – eggs, milk, cheese etc. sliding around like the contents of an ocean liner on rough seas.

Do you remember?

Do you remember that book? I wanted a secret house like that underneath the table – I made one in bed pulling the sheet up over the headboard. Remember – in the attic – the green chenille tablecloth with fringes, shelves in the alcoves, making a library, writing numbers inside the books – *The Little Round House*, *The Adventures of Fairy Fluster*. All the things on the mantelpiece in the bedroom – I'd have to kiss them all goodnight. Chumping for wood on bonfire night. Mischievous Night, leaping around the streets covered in sheets like the Ku-Klux-Klan. The parcels from America mother hated, with comics and chewing gum and give-away matches – and the Mexican felt jacket with the woman on the back. You did a picture of me didn't you? . . . her woollen plaits... In a smocked dress with a Peter Pan collar – from just above the waist – my eyes closed, my face all blue... father's callipers leaning against the wall. The bucket she kept for him under the stairs. Codeine and distalgesic. The fight with mother; father calling Uncle Percy to sort it out. His fat fingers. The staircase. Banging my head against the wall.

Badly worn stair treads can be replaced with hardboard.

Level the worn areas; remove old nails and lumps of paint. Rub over the surface with coarse glass-paper. Pieces of tempered hardboard should be cut to the exact shape of each tread (which may differ slightly in dimension). Each piece may be numbered to indicate which stair it belongs to. Make up a sizeable pot of fairly hot glue; mix with sawdust to form a warm, sticky paste. Apply with a stiff spatula and with a minimum of delay glue the pieces of hardboard in position, securing with panel pins. Three or four longer pins should be driven cautiously through the hardboard covering the worn area, care being taken not to squeeze the paste out with too vigorous a use of the hammer.

The washing is drenched – it's been on the line all night. I'll need an umbrella to bring it in.

How the makings of a house

Brick, stone – seemingly impervious, inanimate, un-breathing – can exude *un-lived-in-ness*. I know as I approach, like knowing when someone's behind you. By closing an eye or turning my head, I can pretend it no longer exists. Suppose I bow my head – a downward view – walk straight past, limit the exposure. Having the desire to avoid is built on prior knowledge. There has to be some seeing – a knowing what it is one doesn't want to. How to un-know? Place or pile on top taking care to cover completely, each layer a little thicker, a little heavier, a little more opaque. Pile upon pile, each with its own peculiarity – a corner not quite aligned, a texture not to the liking; a hole in the weft, one whose hooking back requires too much patience. And so attention is diverted, woe superseded by woe.

Brick can breathe; brick is full of inexactitude, places for the air to enter.

Why concoct?

Just a young mother and her child on the corner of a verandah, a mother who'd lost, as a child, her own young mother, doing as a mother does, the best she could. Your mother's name was Lena: Lena Levy – Lena, *Linda*. Why didn't you tell me? I see the family likeness, here, in this picture of your parents' wedding (sent to me with a family tree twelve pages long): you to Lena and her sister Hilda, my sister and my daughter to you. *Call me Leah Rochal, my Yiddisha name.* I was told you were always wanting. Of course, of course you were! How did Lena die Mama, how did she die? In all your life, I never called you Mama.

What if everything were fixed?

Not as in mended, glued stuck, immovable – though there's something of that – but in time, permanent and unchanging? Where would I place them, my chosen ones? Nanna, always in her kitchen making drop scones on the griddle; my father, his head through a cardboard hole, in a barrel about to be pitched over Niagara Falls, smiling, smiling; Roy in the back garden at Leighton Road, scrubbing old paint off the basket chair with a wire brush …chair upstairs, chair from home, home that jars – red, dull and chipped now, revealing its sickly green. And where would Will be? Pulling rescued bits of train set from a cardboard box – track, signals, broken carriages, engines always fallen out, loving plans to fix them forever in his mind.

It's a mixture of a house:

A scary-deep-in-the-woods-lopsided-rickety-door-shuttered cottage, which isn't what it seems, and a back-to-back. (The best ones are in Edinburgh: stone houses with steps up to a front door halfway up the building, the bottom part being accessible from the back at ground level, which is, I surmise, the front of a different house. So the backs are fronts and the fronts are backs. Or it could be that the house is split in half depth ways though I expect the former is true.) I have done my best to disguise its regularity, but square it is whichever way you look. I'm seeing a corner, a wet fish shop – white brick tiles, houses converging like the tip of a triangle. One side contains a whole terrace, each with a chimney, the farthest house barely visible, not that a fog has fallen; generations reduced to nothing. When I do look inside, climbing a chair to reach it off the shelf, a chair whose legs my father cut down for me (my father with a saw?) I find I've forgotten the children sleeping there three to a bed, the cat (a mere snippet) curled on top, the bed entirely filling the floor, the ceiling reaching right up to the roof: I can almost hear them breathing.

www.ingramcontent.com/pod-product-compliance
Lightning Source LLC
Chambersburg PA
CBHW031159160426
43193CB00008B/433